The Ultimate Audition Book
for Teens Volume III
111 One-Minute Monologues

THE ULTIMATE AUDITION BOOK FOR TEENS SERIES

The Ultimate Audition Book for Teens Volume 1:
111 One-Minute Monologues by Janet Milstein

The Ultimate Audition Book for Teens Volume 2:
111 One-Minute Monologues by L. E. McCullough

The Ultimate Audition Book for Teens Volume 3:
111 One-Minute Monologues by Kristen Dabrowski

The Ultimate Audition Book for Teens Volume 4:
111 One-Minute Monologues by Debbie Lamedman

The Ultimate Audition Book for Teens Volume 5:
111 Shakespeare Monologues

THE ULTIMATE SCENE STUDY SERIES FOR TEENS

The Ultimate Scene Study Series for Teens Volume 1:
60 Shakespeare Scenes

The Ultimate Scene Study Series for Teens Volume 2:
60 Short Scenes by Debbie Lamedman

THE ULTIMATE MONOLOGUE SERIES
FOR MIDDLE SCHOOL ACTORS

The Ultimate Monologue Book for Middle School Actors Volume 1:
111 One-Minute Monologues by Kristen Dabrowski

The Ultimate
Audition Book for Teens
VOLUME III

• • •

111 One-Minute
Monologues

Kristen Dabrowski

YOUNG ACTORS SERIES

A Smith and Kraus Book

A Smith and Kraus Book
Published by Smith and Kraus, Inc.
177 Lyme Road, Hanover, NH 03755
www.smithandkraus.com

Copyright © 2004 by Kristen Dabrowski
All rights reserved.

First Edition: April 2004
Manufactured in the United States of America
9 8 7 6 5 4 3 2

Cover and text design by Julia Gignoux, Freedom Hill Design

Library of Congress Cataloging-in-Publication Data
Dabrowski, Kristen.
The ultimate audition book for teens III : 111 one-minute monologues /
by Kristen Dabrowski —1st ed.
ISBN 1-57525-307-0 (vol. 3)
Summary: A collection of 111 original monologues, all about one minute long, to be
used by male and female teenage actors in auditions.
1. Monologues. 2. Acting. 3. Auditions.
[1. Monologues. 2. Acting—Auditions.] I. Title. II. Young actors series.
PN2080.L36 2003
812'.6—dc21
2002030413

Dedication

To my friends and family, who continually inspire me
and share my adventures.

Contents

Introduction

Hello, actors! As a professional actor for eleven years now, I know how hard the search for the perfect monologue can be. A monologue should be immediate, active, and fun. You shouldn't mind having to say it over and over when you're practicing, auditioning, or performing it. You should be able to relate to it. This can be difficult. Most plays are written for adults. Then where are you supposed to find monologues? This is book for you!

Here are some tips on approaching monologues:

1. Pick the monologue that hits you. Trust your instincts. You'll pick the right one!

2. Make the monologues active. What do you want and how do you try to get it?

3. Who are you talking to and where are they? Some monologues have you speaking to more than one person. Make sure you make this as clear as possible.

4. Do you get answered or interrupted? Be sure to fill in words in your head for the moments when you are spoken to in the monologue, even if it's a simple yes or no.

5. How do you feel about the person or people you are talking to? For example, you speak differently to your best friend than you do to your math teacher.

6. Notes about stage directions and terminology: The stage direction *(Beat.)* or the start of a new paragraph indicates another character is speaking or a new idea is coming up. Stage directions like *(Shocked.)* are suggestions, but do not need to be observed absolutely.

7. Be natural and real. Bring these characters to life as only you can.

Final note: These monologues stand alone as solo pieces (and are not from full-length plays). However, if you want to put together a showcase of monologues, you'll see that some pieces work very well together because they are a continuation of a story line or because they discuss the same subject. Feel free to mix and match.

Enjoy!

Kristen Dabrowski

Female Monologues

• • •

COMEDY

RIGHT TURN OF PASSAGE

SAM

I hate this. I don't want to do this. I know everyone my age does this, but so what? I didn't realize how hard it would be — aah! — to control the — whoa — speed and that you don't need to — what? — okay, okay — turn the wheel very much. Okay. I think I'm getting the hang — whatwhatwhat-what?!?! Oh God! Dad! How could you — dear Lord! I am completely serious. That is not taking the Lord's name in vain 'cause I was actually terrified for my life there, Dad. Turn where? *(Beat.)* Here? Dad, no! Okay, okay — don't yell. Don't yell! I've never done this before! I didn't even want to . . . We are on a major highway. This is way too fast for me! I can't control the speed. *(Beat.)* What? *What? Now?* Aaah!

Dad, we almost *died.* I am *never, never* driving a car. Could you even tell me two seconds *before* we had to make a turn? *(Beat.)* Don't yell at me. Don't even. You are so fired.

ACHIEVING

PAIGE

I want peace on earth. And to be a model. And to graduate from college and become a pediatrician. I am an organ donor. Or I would be, if it came up. I love children. And I promise to be a good role model for children everywhere. And that is why, Mr. Davis, I should be Employee of the Month. I show up on time, too, and do my work in a timely and efficient manner. *(Beat.)* This would look really good on my college application. I could really, really use a raise, too. I'll grovel. I'll be your best friend. *(Beat.)* No, I won't do garbage duty. That's disgusting. Come on! I am model employee and a possible actual model as well, if I get a growth spurt. Which I plan on. Five inches.

Thank you! My picture is going to look so good on this wall. I am going to be the best Employee of the Month ever. I swear.

MY TWO CENTS

AMY

Yeah, what do you want? *(Beat.)* Sorry, sir. What may I get you? *(Beat.)* Listen, maybe my attitude is bad. Have you ever had to stand on your feet for twelve hours, hauling huge trays over your head, walking in and out of a kitchen that's about 150 degrees? I didn't think so. I didn't think you could have or you would have a little more respect for me. Are you really so dumb that you think that all those perky waitresses actually think you're really nice and cute? They want your money.

Hey, I'm just being direct. I don't pull any punches. I'm honest. Probably the only honest waitress you'll ever meet. And maybe you don't like me. Fine. But if you order some time in this century, I'll get your food while it's hot. That's my job. Not flirting with some middle-aged, divorced dude who still wears loafers with no socks. So, let's go back to the beginning. What do you want?

GOOD TIMES

POPPY

He is so out of my league. I am destined to pine in solitude. My love will be unrequited for all time. They say these are the best years of our lives. It has to get better than this. Just has to. Why would anyone like high school? It's scary to think about. I guess those people were, like, the 1 percent of the population who were the beautiful people. And I guess those same people are successful throughout life because we're actually quoting them. Repeating their so-called wise words about this being such a great time in life.

Isn't that the most depressing thought ever? Please don't tell me the most popular people have influence forever and maybe actually have brains. The only thing that gets me through the day is thinking that those people will someday get what's coming to them and the meek will inherit. "We shall overcome" and all that. It's only fair, right?

HAIR DON'T

VICTORIA

Look at this. I can't go. *(Beat.)* My hair! Don't be nice; this is serious! It doesn't look remotely fine! I'm about to "bump into" the hottest guy in school and I cannot go looking like a freak! *(Beat.)* It won't be straight and it won't be curly. It's just a wreck. I hate humidity! It's wrecking everything.

It's fate, isn't it. It's the universe telling me this is not to be. I am being punished for some bad thing I did years ago — that time I cut my sister's hair when I was seven. Bad karma. *(Beat.)* I know I'm overreacting! That's the worst part! I am totally lucid. But here's the thing. I've been planning this and getting my courage up for this *forever*. I promised myself. I made a goal that if I managed to get into shape I would ask Jamie out. This has taken all of my strength to get to this point. And now my hair's ruined it. It's telling me I'm not good enough still. I'm not worthy. *I hate you, horrible hair! I hate you!*

STUCK

FRANCESCA

Glue, okay? I use glue. Does everyone hear that? *I use glue to get my hair like this!*

I am more than my hair. Why is it that no one can comment on anything else in my presence? I do art. I am a photographer. I have lots of interests. Music. I've been to three concerts in the past month. I read! And yet all anyone can ever say is, "What's up with your hair?" "How do you get it to go like that?" "Does it hurt to sleep?" Honestly, you people are so shallow. This hair takes me five minutes to do in the morning. Do you think this is my only statement to the world? And why are people scared of me? Pointy hair equals evil! Beware the devil child!

Your hair isn't so great either. I mean, what is that — a helmet? Why is my hair ugly and yours is great? You look horrible. I should be asking you why you do your hair like that. Is it a perm or did you stick your finger in a light socket? See? See? You don't like it either!

OUCH

KAREN

You look great in that T-shirt. You do. Sexy.

I love your band. Yeah. I heard you at Jane Harper's birthday party. You rocked.

You're wearing sneakers! They are my footwear of choice. Definitely.

So . . . what do you think of me?

I don't know. Like what do you think of what I'm wearing?

"Fine"? Is that the best you can do? I'm trying to seduce you, in case you haven't noticed. You could at least have the courtesy to respond a little. Pretend you are a little interested in what I'm saying, who I am as a person, my appearance.

What planet do you come from? If I came on any stronger, I'd be pregnant! Could you honestly not tell?

Oh. So now you know. So?

Oh my God, I am so embarrassed.

ALTERNATIVES

TARA

I just met the most beautiful man on the dance floor. Over there. *(Beat.)* Yeah, the one with the sparkly mascara. *(Beat.)* He is not gay. I asked. He just likes makeup. Be a little open-minded.

I've always thought one of the best things about being gay must be the ability to share a wardrobe. Can you imagine? And with that guy, Thom, I could have a boyfriend *and* all the advantages of being a lesbian. It's a win-win situation. Think about it. And he's cute, don't you think? Really beautiful. He seems so sweet. *(Beat.)* He's not gay! Honestly, I grilled him on the subject. He said he just likes to wear pretty things. Like a transvestite. They're hetero. Don't you think a guy who thinks about what girls do and what they think is going to be a more sensitive, cool person to be around?

I don't know. Maybe I'm crazy. But it makes sense to me. I like him. I'm going for it. I may regret it later, but I live in the moment.

GRUDGE

GRACE

You did not just touch me. You did not. Oh my God. I am going to have to shower forever now. Did I ever give you any indication that you could touch me? No. No, I didn't. I don't like you. *(Beat.)* This is not playing hard to get. Read my lips: *I don't like you.*

I am not holding a grudge. I mean, yes. I am and I'm not. *(Beat.)* I am still disgusted by the incident in the gym. Don't pretend you don't know what I'm talking about. The one where . . . Fine. You're going to make me say it. The one where you pulled down my gym shorts.

Yes, that was in sixth grade. Duh. I was there, dork. Anyhow, I am still mad at you for that. But that is not the only reason why you disgust me. You disgust me because . . . you just do!

You are not going to kiss me. No, you're not. No — oh, okay. Whatever.

WHY ME

BRIANA

How come no one ever likes me? I'm smart, funny, not ugly. I mean, even ugly people have boyfriends. I've seen them.

Except, gross guys approach me. Today, some guy walked past me and said "Nice tits." What is that? Was that a compliment? I don't think so. I think it was meant to make me feel bad about myself, to make me feel small. And humiliated. And terrible enough to think that gross guy was the best I can do.

So maybe that's my problem. I think I'm better than that tits man. The male persons who pay attention to me are all disgusting rejects. Maybe someday I'll have to face it and settle.

But today is not that day. Maybe the day before the prom. Maybe *that* day I'll be desperate enough to smile and giggle at that vile slob. *(Beat.)* Oh God. I fear that day!

FALLBACK

RITA

The prom is the most important event of our lives. Ever! Learning to walk doesn't compare. Can we agree on this point? *(Beat.)* Okay. So, this is the most important event of our lives to date and I don't even have a date. And I can't find this dress I want that's in this magazine.

You are so lucky you have Kyle. Even if he's not your first choice, you'll have *someone* to go with. A fallback. Like applying to an Ivy League school but knowing you'll get into state college if nothing else works out. Kyle is your state college. And like state college, not bad. Stable. Honest. Trustworthy. *There* when you need it. Attractive, if not lush and perfectly groomed. At this point, I'd consider a community college. Night school. *Anything.*

No. Not Brian. No. I'm not that desperate yet. I know he likes me. He's a GED program. For people who had to drop out of second grade because they live in the mountains and got snowed in and haven't had hot water for the past ten years. I'm mean, I know. *(Beat.)* Can I have Kyle if you don't want him?

PUMPING UP

RHONDA

(Working out.) Why am I doing this? *(Beat.)* It's simple — revenge. That loser pig of a boyfriend must pay for cheating on me. I was so good to him. So I must make him feel pain and remorse. This seemed like the best way to do it. Get in shape. Look hot so he'll be so sorry he ever wronged me and let me go. Pig. He'll pay. Plus, it has the added benefit of making me attractive to others, giving me more energy, and *(Punching the air.)* releasing my anger! That pig!

I still have a way to go before I'm, like, Catherine Zeta-Jones hot, but I'm getting there. And I will make it. I have to. I just want to see him stunned and aroused by my magnificence.

Before I started doing this, I felt worthless and had uncontrollable anger, like the Hulk. Now, I feel great. I highly recommend it. And if anyone *ever* does me wrong again, I will kick their ass!

EX . . . LAX

RAIN

Hi, want a cookie? I made them myself. Just for you. *(Beat.)* Why? Because you're a very special person. I like you lots.

No, I don't hold a grudge. Why would I do that? Because we went out a few times and it didn't work out? Please. That was so minor. At least to me. *(Beat.)* I mean, do you have any . . . feelings for me? No? Then we're fine, right?

So. Have a little cookie. Go on. They're good. *(Beat.)* That's right. Mmmm. Have more.

That should make you feel regular. *(Beat.)* What does that mean? That means those cookies — keep eating — are chockful of delicious laxatives.

Have a nice day!

CUT LOOSE

SERENA

Don't even play me like that. No. No. No. No. You are not talking; I am talking here. Don't even interrupt me. No. No. No. No. You will listen. *(Beat.)* Because I am your girlfriend, that's why. Because I told you to. Do you want to ever see me again? Do you want to keep your reputation? Because I can destroy it like *that* and you know it. *(Beat.)* I can tell people how you cried when I said I would break up with you. I still might. Keep it up, mister. Keep it up. You are dead to me. Get out of my face now, crybaby. *(Beat.)* No. No. No. No. I need a man. I don't need you. Get your sorry, flat butt away from me now.

You heard me.

FAT CHANCE

KIM

This is cellulite, isn't it? I am way too young for this. What did I do to deserve this? If I look like this now, what am I going to look like at forty?

I always wanted to be in those "fabulous at forty" ads. Until today, I thought I would get better with the years. Let's face it, up to now the years haven't been great. I've had glasses, braces, zits, been fat — now this. This is way beyond baby fat.

Only being very, very rich will save me. I need to be Julia Roberts or something. Only I never will because — the cellulite! So, I have to marry some ugly rich guy like Donald Trump. I don't think I could. Those moles, that hair! I'm doomed. Without mega bucks I can't have the hot seaweed wrap to shrink my lumpy fat!

Exercise? You've got to be joking. Pass me the Chunky Monkey. I need to console myself.

DEFENSE

SCARLETT

To overpower your attacker, you want to quickly, instinctively go after certain body parts. Eyes, palm to the nose, fist to the throat. If you're wearing heels, slam them into the bridge of a foot. Knees are vulnerable. As is the groin area. Be active. Be vigilant. Never let an attacker take you to another location. Then you're screwed.

Okay, let's do a little work here. Today our volunteer is Kevin. Thank you for coming today, Kevin. You're doing a wonderful thing for womankind. *(Beat.)* Bernice, will you join Kevin up here? *(Beat.)* Okay, Kevin. Attack Bernice. *(Beat.)* No, really. Go ahead. Bernice can take care of herself, can't you Bernice? Go ahead, Kevin.

Oh, God, Kevin! Are you okay? Bernice, well done! Excellent work! Kevin? *(Beat.)* Kevin? You are wearing a cup, aren't you?

TOO MANY FISH IN THE SEA

CHARLIZE

I have to stay with Chad. I have to. *(Beat.)* I don't even know if things would ever work out with Jeff. I hardly know him. *(Beat.)* It's just that we have such great conversations. I can't help thinking, "What if?" But I can't risk it. It could be a terrible mistake and where would that leave me? Having lost two great guys and being totally alone. *(Beat.)* Well, sure, I'd have you, you're my best friend, but I'd have no boyfriend. I'm not one of those girls who can go without a boyfriend. I get so lonely. I'm not a strong person.

Plus, why should I? This might sound egotistical, but I don't need to. I have Chad. And he's crazy about me. He tells me so all the time. I just can't hurt him. He's so terrific. *(Beat.)* And . . . still . . . there's Jeff. There's an undeniable attraction.

Listen, Deb, would it really be so awful to go on one date with Jeff that Chad wouldn't know about? I wouldn't *do* anything and maybe then I'd know if I should really be with Jeff instead.

Why is life so hard? Why are there so many decisions to make? And so many adorable boys to choose from?

BAR NONE

SHANNON

Yeah, I'm twenty-one and my friend here is twenty-two. People always tell us we look young. It's kind of embarrassing. We used to be gymnasts, so we're short for our age. But we're totally mature. *(Beat.)* My birthday? Oh, April 27th. *(Beat.)* What year? That's a strange question. Can't you do the math? I don't mean to make you feel stupid, but it's totally obvious that I was born in nineteen . . . eighty . . . one. *(Beat.)* What do you mean "wrong"? I think I'd know the year I was born.

Of course that would make me twenty-three. That's how old I said I was. Now can you just let me in so I can meet up with my twenty-five-year-old boyfriend who was born in nineteen eighty-three? I mean, nineteen eighty — seventy-nine? He's going to buy me a beer and we are going to dance in an adult, mature way. Like the lambada, maybe.

I am offended! I mean . . . flattered since you think I am so young. Are you hitting on me? How old do you think I am anyway? *(Beat.)* Fourteen? Now that is just insulting. Excuse me. My friend and I going to find a cool club with a smart doorman now who knows that a twenty-one year old woman was born in nineteen eighty . . . Whatever! Let's go, Amanda.

DEVELOPING COMPLEXES

GEORGEANNE

It's weird how it happened. I thought it would be the end of my life. I did. You know how things are when you're a kid. Everything is so important. And you think everyone is looking at you. What am I saying, I still feel that way! Anyhow, I wanted to disappear. Forever.

Then something so — unbelievable — happened. I still don't really understand it. Some people, some girls, thought it was cool. That I developed so early. Here I was, not quite eleven, the only girl who *needed* a bra. I was trying to wear baggy clothes and pretend it never happened, and they were dying to catch up. I guess the grass is always greener . . . *(Beat.)* We have to spend the rest of our lives dealing with this crap. Why would you ever want to start early? They're just these — things — attached to me. How did they get there? Why? You have no idea how awful gym class can be.

I'm totally jealous. I wish I was a man. Now *you* have got it good. Except for those dangling penis things. I don't quite get that.

PARTS OF ME

SUMMER

You men and your thingamajigs. It's absurd. We've got things, too, women, but we don't go around all day and night thinking about our things. *(Beat.)* Okay, okay, we think about our stuff — are they big enough, do they bounce too much, are they saggy, is so-and-so looking at them — but it isn't so all consuming. *(Beat.)* Okay, maybe at certain times, in certain places, wearing certain clothes, they can become a prominent focus. But let's face it; our protruding things aren't as weird as yours. I don't know how you sit.

Our things are not weird! *(Beat.)* That is so gross. They are not milk makers. They're . . . well, yes, but . . . That is really weird. And disturbing. I don't know what I'd do if milk . . . oh my God, that is the grossest thing ever.

I hope you're happy. I'm a freak!

DOS AND DON'TS

VIVICA

I'm making a list of things I'll never do again, so I don't forget. Never will I drink orange juice after brushing my teeth. Mint and orange do *not* go together. Never will I wear a strapless bra and dance. Never will I attempt to improvise a phone call with someone I like. Never drive with Dad in the passenger seat. Never watch those forensic shows right before bed.

There are no clear answers, though, about what I should do. That part really has me stumped. It's funny. It's somewhat clear to see what other people ought to do. Who they might be in the future. What clothes they shouldn't wear. But when it's you, everything gets so fuzzy. But we're supposed to figure it out for ourselves. How come? That takes so long. Why don't I just ask you? *(Beat.)* What should I do with my life? Do these pants make me look fat?

GOTTA GO

EMILIA

Excuuuse me? Is anyone in there? Listen, I know you're in there. *(Beat.)* Maybe you think this is funny, but I really have to go to the bathroom. I've been waiting for, like, ten minutes now. *(Beat.)* Are you, um, sick? Should I call someone? *(Beat.)* My God, what is your problem? Do you think you're the most important person in the world? Well, news flash, you're not. *(Beat.)* I drank a cranberry juice and three diet cokes. I've been dancing for HOURS. Jumping up and down. I have to *go*. This is *serious*.

I can see your shoes! And, by the way, they are not very nice. Man-shoes. They make your legs look fat!

I'm sorry. I didn't mean that. Really. I'm in distress. I don't know what I'm saying. *(Beat.)* Give me a break. Please. Please. I'm begging you. I am going to pee my pants. And they are *new*. Wait. *(Beat.)* Oh, my God. They *are* men's shoes, aren't they? And, and — there's two of you in there! Oh my God, you're — *doing it*, aren't you? Oh — my — God. This place is filthy! Have some dignity. I can't believe — in public? Um, could you — are you almost — *I have to go! Get out!*

GOOD ADVICE

NINA

Let me give you some advice. Track. Lacrosse will get you a broken nose or a knee operation, not to mention all the running. *(Beat.)* No, that's where you're wrong. You don't run that much in track. Work with me, okay? We go out to run in the woods and on the local streets. Right? Who's around? Just us. Only two or three people actually like to run and they know if they told anyone we'd kill them.

Here's another tip: hurdles. I have gotten a varsity letter since my freshman year thanks to hurdles. And I am not the least bit athletic. Not even a little. No one does hurdles. Just Amy and me. Amy is good. She gets first place. I am terrible. I come in second or third, if another school has a hurdler, too, which they usually don't. I get in the newspaper and everything. I knock almost all of them down and take, like, twenty minutes to finish the course. But it doesn't matter. I'm in second place *bam* like that. And you don't ever vomit like the runners do. Easy. When I cross that finish line, I do a little victory lap, arms in the air, running in slo-mo, like a movie. It's really funny. 'Cause I suck.

Hurdles. And don't tell anyone else or you'll blow the whole thing.

BAD CALL

BRITT

Are you okay?

I didn't mean to. I think she's hurt! Competition just gets the best of me. Seriously, I am totally sorry. It looks like her nose is broken. Yuck! What should we do?

No, coach, you can't take me out of the game. It's not my fault. It's the game's fault. Maybe girls shouldn't brandish sticks. I was just doing my job; holding up my part for the team. *(Beat.)* I'm the best player! This is suicide. Listen, I'll do whatever you want. I'll visit that girl, whoever she is, in the hospital. Believe me, I didn't mean for it to happen. And this is a pivotal game for us.

You are making the biggest mistake of your life! Her nose was ugly to begin with!

THE PERILS OF MINISKIRTS

MEG

Thanks for visiting me, Lily. It hurts. I don't know why people would do this on purpose. It's not just my nose that hurts; everything hurts. I move my big toe and you can't imagine the pain I feel.

So, tell me the truth. I can see it in your face. I'm a hideous freak, aren't I? This is the most normal I've looked for weeks. Who knew my life would end at fifteen? And all because I played field hockey, the most unwatched and unrewarding sport ever. It's not like you can win a gold medal in it or anything. *(Beat.)* You think so? I've never heard of an Olympic field hockey team. Well, still, I'm never going to play it again. I just got into it in the first place because I thought the skirts were cute.

Well, tennis has short skirts, too. And much more distance between the players. I've got to pick up the pieces of my ruined life and move on. Plus, there are lots of shiny tennis awards to be won.

Thanks for visiting. I feel so much better now!

THE GOOD OLDE DAYS

TANYA

I'd love to live back when women wore big, beautiful dresses. Everyone was so much more civilized. They went to balls and danced the night away. Can you imagine, Zoë? So romantic. Men were chivalrous and thought about what they said and did, trying to woo women. Oh, to be wooed! Kissed on the hand. Loads of sweet talk. Those were the days.

They did not throw pee and crap out the windows! Come on. That's nasty.

I don't believe you! You would not pee in a pot in the middle of a room. Well, I know they didn't have indoor plumbing, but they had dignity!

So what if they got married young. *(Beat.)* Well, I could marry an older man. Sure. There are lots of hot guys who are older than me. Practically everyone on TV and in the movies is older than us. I could marry one of them. *(Beat.)* No, I wouldn't marry someone my dad's age or someone ugly. I wouldn't have to. I would be rich and beautiful.

Why? Because I said so. Why do you have to be such a pig, Zoë? Can't I just have my one romantic dream without you crapping it up?

WORSHIP ME

MAURA

I've always wanted to have a guy paint my toenails. Don't know why. It's not like I have some kind of foot-fetish thing. It's more like it's romantic somehow. And powerful. He's doing for you. You just get to sit back and watch him serve you. It must have been great to be a queen. *(Beat.)* Sure, yeah, there are queens still but it's not the same. Besides, I'm certainly not the next in line for any throne. I think it would have come up by now. But how funny would that be? "Maura Finkelman, the royal family of England all just went crazy at once. It's a national crisis. You, Miss Finkelman, (or should I say Your Majesty) happen to be the next in line for the throne."

First thing I'd do? Get some servants to cook for me and do my laundry. *(Beat.)* They wouldn't be slaves! Please, I'd hire them. Pay them a salary. But I wouldn't have to do anything I didn't want to do anymore. And I'd get some stud to paint my toenails. *(Beat.)* I would. So would you. Don't deny it.

DEEP THOUGHTS

CHLOE

Argh! I hate these perfume samples in magazines. They are so nasty. I have a really acute sense of smell. I can't stand anything that smells unclean. Why do unscented deodorants smell like sweat? It makes no sense. And why would anyone want to smell like musk? It makes you smell like a French whore. Why do people say that anyway? Are French whores any stinkier than whores from other countries?

Do you think there's life on other planets? And how come those aliens on *Star Trek* all have different faces but they still have all the same body parts? Like none of them have tentacles instead of legs. *(Beat.)* I said tentacles, not testicles.

Honestly. You need to start thinking serious thoughts and having opinions about the world, Lori.

HOT MAMA

DANICA

Summer is not all it's cracked up to be. It's hot. You have to wear shorts and tank tops. I hate shorts. I feel like my butt is hanging out of the bottom of them for a good two weeks before I get used to them. You have to shave all the time. God, I hate that. You have to think about which bra you wear because otherwise the straps will show depending on which shirt you put on. Give me cold weather, sweaters, layers, long pants anytime! Don't even get me started on swimwear. We could be here for weeks.

Oh God, they're coming over. Try to look casual. Try to look like you're not sweating and your armpits don't stink.

HOG HEAVEN

BROOKE

You call this being a friend? Being supportive? We are a mess. We are losers! I hate us. Here we are at a café, having polished off a piece of chocolate cake *each*! À la mode, no less! What's wrong with us?

And all the while, as we stuff our faces, we talk about how we're fat and we never get dates and no one likes us — duh! How can we be so retarded? No, sorry. That is a total insult to retarded people. They have way more sense than us.

We are so screwed up. How can we stop the cycle? Why is eating so damn much fun? It just feels so chummy, so friendly.

Why isn't jogging fun? It's just not. I don't know how we can be expected to be social and thin at the same time. It's totally unrealistic.

COFFEE AND HUMILIATION

KELLY

Oh my God. You know how that old Indian guy behind the counter kind of freaks me out? Did I not tell you that? *(Beat.)* Well, one day he starts singing Indian love songs to me. Telling me how they are so beautiful. It's was totally embarrassing and weird.

So, today I go in there and I'm ordering. Trying to be unfriendly so he won't start singing or anything. So, everything's going fine. I'm not even making eye contact. And I go to pay. $2.43. And I've got a twenty. I hand him my bill and he says, "Singles?" So, I'm like, "Are you asking me if I'm single? 'Cause I'm not!" And he says, "Do you have any singles? Instead of a twenty dollar bill?" Color me mortified. I could not have been more humiliated. But it gets worse!

This guy, instead of seeing my revulsion at thinking he's hitting on me, he thinks I have a crush on him or something. He gets this goofy smile on his face. So now I can never go back there. Even though it's the closest coffee shop from my house. Gross.

THIS STINKS

INDIRA

I'm not going to school. You can't make me. I feel like bugs are crawling all over me. My hair is sticking to my face. I feel greasy and my legs are stubbly. Old sweat from yesterday is stuck to me. No way.

Until we have hot water, I am not leaving this house. *(Beat.)* If there were a fire, *maybe* I'd leave. But otherwise, no. Spending hours like this is inhuman. I'm a beast.

I am a strong person. I can take criticism, even mocking. But this . . . you can't make me. *(Beat.)* This may sound crazy, but I actually like school most of the time. I'm a good student. I get along with people mostly. But filth I cannot take.

Give me a break and let me get my own way just this once. *(Beat.)* Remember what I was younger and you'd nag me to take a bath? See how I've grown as a human being? You should be proud of me. How I take pride in my appearance and have good hygiene habits. Good kid raising, Mom. Way to go!

I will be telling my therapist about this years from now. You know that?

PACKING

JILL

Are you packing your stuffed animals? What do you think other people do? It's college and it means we're becoming adults. So . . . no?

But I want to keep Oliver the Otter with me! He's been my faithful companion for so many years.

But . . . we will be independent and there's a possibility of having guys in our rooms, so we don't want to look like little kids. So . . . no. The critters stay at home.

Except . . . I've never spent a night without Oliver. He's warded off evil spirits for eighteen years now. He's listened to my every problem. Leaving him here with my parents might actually be dangerous. What if he starts blabbing? I don't know that I can trust him alone here with so many deep, dark secrets.

Like what? None of your business! Don't ask him — he works for me. Give him to me now. Oliver — you're going to college!

Female Monologues

· · ·

DRAMA

LEAVING

AMBER

Mom, where are we going? *(Beat.)* What do you mean, you don't know? Just leaving? Where's Dad? *(Beat.)* He's not coming. So . . . you're leaving him. We're leaving him. What if I don't want to leave him? *(Beat.)* I can, too, stay with him. He loves me and I love him. I don't mind that he drinks. I'll make him stop. He can stop. We have to give him time.

Please, Mom, don't do this. I . . . I know he gets . . . bad. And it's scary. *(Beat.)* I know I said I hated him, too. But I don't. I didn't. I was just . . . embarrassed. He loves us. And he's all we have. You don't have a job. We can't do this alone. I don't want to go to a new school. Can't you think this over again? Please, Mom!

You only think of yourself! This is my life, too!

MISUNDERSTOOD

ELLE

My chest feels so tight. I think I'm going to burst. I don't think I've ever been this angry in my life. Oh! I hate how I start to cry when I'm mad. How come I can't just let it out? *(Beat.)* You don't have to answer that. I know the answer. I'm so afraid of people not liking me, even when I don't like them, that I just can't confront anyone. I hate that about myself. Sometimes I just hate myself.

No, I know I shouldn't hate myself. I should hate my mom. I just can't be what she wants. And I can't tell her. She doesn't hear me, even when I try. But she's my mom. I live with her. I love her. But I really can't stand her. She has no idea who I am.

SUGAR DADDY

CARLA

Can you really blame me? He's got a gorgeous car, wears the best clothes, takes me to the nicest places . . . It really doesn't matter that he's older. It makes it better, actually. He knows things. He's nice to me. Knows how to treat a woman. He likes me because I'm young, maybe, but also because of who I am. I'm livelier than the other women he's dated. He told me that.

Anyone who tells you that money doesn't matter, they're lying. It does matter. Why would I ever want to go out with some high school boy who treats me like crap and takes me to a burger joint when I can get dressed up and go to a hotel restaurant? There's no comparison. Someday you'll understand. And if you ask me, you're jealous anyhow. I've got everything you or any other girl could want and I've got it *now*. I don't have to wait until I'm in college or in my twenties. My dreams are coming true *today*.

THE WORST MISTAKE I EVER MADE

ELIZA

It feels like I went from one trap to another sometimes. Went from living with my dad to living here with Henry. My father tried to tell me this was a mistake, but you never listen to your father, do you? But it is really . . . tempting to let someone else take care of everything. Henry handles everything. I can just relax. It's comforting to surrender, let your guard go down.

Sometimes, though, I feel like I'm slipping away. I'm bored so much I want to scream. And I don't know who I am anymore. Everything I do is for Henry or with Henry.

I don't have any other friends anymore. But if I left Henry, not only would that be admitting my dad is right, I'd also be totally alone. So I guess I'll stick with him. He loves me. He takes care of me.

HARBORING THOUGHTS

LIBERTY

(Arms in the attitude of the Statue of Liberty throughout.)

Athens. I said *Athens*! I said *warm*! I saw myself in the country-side, looking out over the blue, *blue* Mediterranean. Not the *gray* New York Harbor!

I didn't even want to leave home, to be honest. I was comfortable. A little cold in only a robe, but I was comfortable. Everything I was used to was taken from me. Completely alone for the first time in my life. It's scary. You feel empty. Everything drops away. And all you can think about is how hard it is and how lonely you are. *(Beat.)* Time does make it better. But part of me always misses what was. When I didn't worry about the weather or rusting or growing older.

This is starting to get comfortable. But would I give it up to go home? In a second. Ignorance *is* bliss. If anyone told me I'd be raised only to be sent away, I wouldn't have been nearly as happy. But — I am loved. It makes things better, knowing that. At night, when I'm most alone, I try to *feel* it, remember it, to get myself through. And in the day, especially in February, I look into the sun and dream of Greece.

LIFE LESSONS

LOUISA

No, I don't want a drink. I gave up beer and pickled herring when I was ten. *(Beat.)* No, honestly, that's all that was ever in my dad's refrigerator. I'd get back from riding my bike, I'd be so hot, and so I'd have a beer. It was cold; I didn't even care what it tasted like. And my dad didn't notice. *(Beat.)* I didn't even think it was bad; I thought everybody just drank whatever was in the fridge. You don't know what drunk is until you've had two beers on a steaming hot day and you're only eighty pounds. It's not good. Wouldn't recommend it.

Anyhow, I'm actually an orphan now. Isn't it weird? I don't mean to be flip about it; it really is kinda terrible, but I just never thought it was possible. It's like something out of a book. *(Beat.)* I guess my foster family is nice. They are nice. I like them. But it's strange. Because they haven't completely claimed me. So I always feel like I'm on trial. There's no room for mistakes, which is hard. Everybody makes mistakes. So when I do, I have to try and hide them. But it's best not to make them at all. So no beer and pickled herring, thank you, from here on in.

TRUST ME

ARIANNA

How am I ever supposed to trust myself again? I have the worst judgment about people. I must or I'd never make such a mistake. He is a total creep and I had no idea. It's just that, he seemed so sincere. Meanwhile, he's still going out with Liza at the same time. I am the world's biggest sucker. He promised he wasn't and I believed him. I am so mad at myself I could just die.

Suz, he's the first guy who ever asked me out. Maybe no one will again. Especially when they hear that he preferred that troll to me. She's not even pretty! *(Beat.)* I wish it didn't upset me so much! I wish I didn't like him. But the worst part is, I still do. How can you hate someone and like them at the same time?

GUY SANE

CALLIE

I just can't be all full of angst when it comes to guys. It's against my nature. Why should I care what they think, if they like me? *(Beat.)* I'm not saying it doesn't matter at all or that I'll never care, but I just can't get all wrapped up in it. *(Beat.)* That's not true! Is it? I do not scare them away. I'm an independent person with opinions. If some guy can't respect a girl because she has a brain and opinions, then that guy is not for me. What a wimp. *(Beat.)* What do you mean, that kind of talk is exactly what you mean? Honestly, if I'm supposed to be an empty-headed little idiot to get boys to like me . . . I just can't play like that. *(Beat.)* Oh, all right. I suppose I could . . . soften my approach a little. But not if someone makes me angry. Not around macho jerks.

Yeah. I do get scared sometimes. That I'll be alone. That I'll never have any normal social life. I mean, there are kids who are thirteen who've had actual *relationships* and I haven't even had a date. *(Beat.)* Don't tell anyone I told you that. Any of this. I know you think I'm nuts, but it's important for me to feel strong and independent.

DECISIONS, DECISIONS

JOY

I think I'm going to grow it again. I don't know.

People think girls with short hair are tough or lesbians. I'm not. I don't love pink and I think most boys are stupid, but I'm not a lesbian. It's awful the way people jump to conclusions. I mean, I don't see someone with glasses and think they're smart or someone with a leather jacket and think they're cool or someone with big breasts and think they're dumb — okay, I do think that. But it's not fair that I think that and I punish, *punish* myself for that kind of small thinking. I'm a monster.

But, anyway, I got off the subject, what I was going to say is that if I grow my hair it's not because I feel pressured to by society or boys, it's because I miss that feeling. *(Beat.)* How can I describe it? That feeling when you have a ponytail all day long and it's so tight that by eight o'clock you're starting to get a headache and you take it out and — wow. *That* feeling. Like your head's melting. Like your brain can finally relax. That smooth feeling. Everything's going to be okay.

With short hair, you get fickle, jaded. You get that free, breezy, easy feeling all the time. Hmmm, this may take some more thought.

HOLDING ON

DARRAH

Austin, you mean so much to me. This is our one-month anniversary. Do you want to go celebrate? *(Beat.)* What do you mean you have somewhere else to be? You have to start being honest now. I know we got off to a bad start, but things have been so good recently. *(Beat.)* I know we fight, but we're both passionate people. That's a good thing.

That time away last week really helped us, I think. I'm so glad you suggested we take some space. I needed you to see how much I meant to you.

I know you went out with Lisa. I guess you had to get that out of your system. But I know it meant nothing. How could it? We're meant to be together. And now we are. It feels so good to be alone again. Just the two of us. *(Beat.)* Come on, you don't *really* have to go now, do you? *(Beat.)* So what is this "stuff" you have to do? Lisa? The class slut? *(Beat.)* Go ahead; go then. But if you walk away this time, I will never, never take you back. Never. Not like last time. Never.

THE FIRST

GABRIELLE

I do want to. I really do. You know how much I like you. *(Beat.)* Try to be a little understanding. I'm just not ready. I want to make a good decision, not just a hormonal one.

This is a *huge* decision. Think about the worst-case scenario. I could get pregnant. You could have a disease and give it to me. *(Beat.)* Okay, fine. You don't have a disease, but how can I know that? *(Beat.)* Fine. Forget that part. *(Beat.)* Condoms break. People get pregnant anyway. *(Beat.)* I know that won't *necessarily* happen, but I want to be sure. Can't you understand that? *(Beat.)* I know it's hard for you. It's hard for me, too. It really is. I really like you. You make me really happy.

Please. Please just be a little bit patient. *(Beat.)* I know you already have been. Just a little while longer. *(Beat.)* Are you giving me an ultimatum? I never thought you were that kind of person. Why are you doing this to me?

YOU DON'T WANNA KNOW

MANDY

Why won't you look at me? Do I disgust you? Are you thinking of someone else? It's Bianca, isn't it?

I could have your baby, too, you know. I'm just too smart for that. But that's what you like. Someone who's needy; someone who depends on you. It's not fair. It won't work out with her.

Why is the timing always wrong? What do I have to do to finally get you to myself? If I got pregnant, would you drop everything for me? *(Beat.)* I bet you wouldn't. You said you cared about me, but now you're just walking away. How can you be like that? How can you be such a jerk? I will not take it easy. I'm mad. I have a right to be.

YOU PROBABLY THINK THIS MONOLOGUE IS ABOUT YOU

JULES

You represent everything I hate. You're vain, full of yourself. You can't pass a mirror without looking. You obsessively touch your hair if there's the slightest breeze — and forget about the rain! You're not all that. *(Beat.)* Don't pretend like you don't know what I'm talking about. That's bullshit. Let's be real. You are so sure you're irresistible. One minute you talk about your girlfriend, next minute you're hitting on my friend, then the next minute you're telling me how cute I look. Did it ever occur to you that this makes me feel worse, not better? You'd hit on anyone; therefore, I'm not special. *(Beat.)* Oh, sure, I thought you were a little cute for the first, oh, ten seconds after I met you. But I'm over you. *So* very over you.

GIRL GONE WILD

AMBER

You want me to what? *(Beat.)* And you're going to film it? Who's going to see this film?

You think I'm hot? You're pretty cute, too, actually. *(Beat.)* Oh my God, I've totally had too much to drink, haven't I? No offense. I mean, this is actually sounding like a good idea! Yeah, it is a classic spring break thing to do.

Okay, okay. You don't have to be pushy about it, mister. God. *(Beat.)* I'm thinking about it, okay? *(Beat.)* You don't have to get abusive. I'm not a prude. *(Beat.)* No, I don't think I want a drink to loosen up. I'm plenty loose. Is that camera on? 'Cause I'm ready for my close-up, mister.

BACK HOME

NIVA

I'm fine. The same person you used to know. Not any different. So let's just act like it never happened. I'd rather not talk about it anyway. *(Beat.)* I guess it affected me a little. It's not exactly normal to be kidnapped. I did something stupid, meeting that guy from the Net. Whatever. No big deal. *(Beat.)* Are you really going to make me talk about this? God, let's get it over with, then. I just thought, you know, adults do this all the time. Make a date with someone they meet online. And it just went bad.

Look, I really don't want to talk about this. *(Beat.)* What do you mean, "I should"? What do you know about it? I'll tell you what you know — nothing. He was a jerk and it was bad and that's all I'm going to say about it. I'm still the same person inside and I'd appreciate it if you and everyone could just treat me that way. Not like I'm some nut or someone you have to be extra-careful with. I'm the same person I always was. *(Beat.)* If you're my friend, you'll just shut up now. Okay?

MORE

KALEIGH

Why are you looking at me like that? Just because I talked about God? *(Beat.)* Why is everyone so afraid of religion? It's been around for zillions of years and most people, when they're pressed to answer, say they believe in God. So how come we can't talk about it? We spend, like, twenty-four hours a day thinking about shopping and who's dating which football player. Can't we take twenty minutes to discuss something serious?

What if there is a God? He must be pissed that we never think about anything *real*. Or if there is no God, what then? And if God is a woman, why do we get cramps? I mean, world wars are waged over religion. Shouldn't we know a little something about it? Don't you ever think maybe you ought to be informed about things rather than just accepting what you're told?

PURGING

MARISA

Stop eating! Just stop it! You disgust me. Seriously. First, you eat nothing but vitamins and granola for days on end, then you eat an entire pizza on your own. You clearly have an eating disorder. "Disorder" — what an understatement! You're a full-scale mess. *(Beat.)* Why are you so damn proud of it? It's nasty! Do you know what it's like to watch you pig out and throw up? It's not cute when you tell me whether eggs come up easy or not.

You're vile. *(Beat.)* I don't care if it changes your life or not, me saying this. I know nothing I say will probably make a difference. But I can't feel sorry for you and overlook this anymore. I can't be your friend and support this any longer.

CHANGES

MEREDITH

I just thought she'd be in my life forever. I think about her all the time, even now. It just seems impossible that my best friend, someone the same age as me, could be dead. I still expect to see her in school. Every time something funny happens, I turn around to share a look with her. Because she'd always understand. We always thought the same stuff was funny.

Now it's like I'm the new kid at school. She's the only one I ever really hung around with. I didn't need other friends. And now I have to go back there. I don't know anyone anymore. I don't know what to do. There's no one else like her. I'm going to be all alone from now on. *(Beat.)* Don't feel sorry for me, Mom. Don't. I just have to get used to it. And I will. I'll be independent from now on.

SOLITARY CONFINEMENT

DARIA

Can I sit here? There's nowhere else. Sorry. *(Beat.)* So, how come you're sitting by yourself? Everyone thinks I'm a stuck-up bitch. That's why I'm sitting by myself.

It's stupid. I'm a dancer and I travel a lot with the ballet. So it's hard to make friends in school. Everyone thinks that I'm full of myself. I think they're jealous. Because I'm pretty and thin and talented. *(Beat.)* I guess that makes me sound like a bitch! But I don't mean to. It's a fact.

I could pretend that I think I'm stupid and worthless, but I'm not. I have a future ahead of me. I know just what I'm going to be and who I am. I was just born that way. And I don't see why I should be cursed for being sure of myself. Why I should pretend to be less than I am? It's not right. I'd rather be by myself than be a "regular" person. *(Beat.)* You should do the same. You're smarter than these losers. Don't stoop to their level. Ever.

INSIDE MY SKIN

SONYA

You don't know how I feel. No one here knows how I feel. Do you know what it's like to be the only person of color in the entire school, the entire community? You don't, and you never will. Even if you try to imagine it, you can't. I'm always watching to make sure I don't make waves, trying to fit in.

I'm keenly aware of how I'll never have what you have. I'll never be able to make the cheerleading team and not wonder if I'm just the token. In the same situation, you assume that you're just the most talented person. Do you see the difference? I always have to wonder at people's motives. And I have to try to ignore half the things people say when they're not thinking. Otherwise I'd be mad all the time.

Don't you think it made me mad the other day when you made fun of how that girl talked at the mall the other day? *(Beat.)* Oh, please, you know what I'm talking about. She was black. And from the city. You said you couldn't understand a word she said and why can't people learn to speak English. Maybe she doesn't have the advantages you have. Maybe you shouldn't be critical when you have no idea what you're talking about. *(Beat.)* I know you're not trying to be rude, Ginny, but maybe you ought to step inside someone else's shoes once in a while.

POWER PLAY

MICHELLE

Okay. You've made yourself clear. I'm a freshman and you're a senior. Fine. But here's the thing. I don't care. And this has to stop. I went along with this charade for long enough. Just because you're older than me doesn't mean you get to tell me what to do and call me names. I played along to be a good sport for a while now. Can't we move on?

Are you serious? You "have it out" for me. What does that mean? You're going to beat me up? *(Beat.)* What for? What did I ever do to you other than being born four years later?

I thought this was just a joke. *(Beat.)* Yeah, I guess I am scared. No one's ever hated me before. And I really don't see why you should. *(Beat.)* "Because"? That's your reason? *(Beat.)* After school today? Tell me you're kidding!

CAST OUT

NICOLE

Excuse me, Mrs. Sweeney? Hi. Can I talk to you a minute? *(Beat.)* I wanted to talk to you about the casting. *(Beat.)* No, to be honest. I'm not excited about it. It's my senior year, Mrs. Sweeney. My last chance. I've been in every play since my freshman year. I've done chorus, I've stage managed, I've painted the set. I've been *involved*. And I never complained about anything because I thought this would be my chance. This would be my year. *(Beat.)* Yeah, I see I've got a part, but . . . it's the wrong part. Completely wrong.

I wanted to be Laurie. I can sing that part. I know all the songs. I've listened to *Oklahoma* since I was a little girl. I was born to play that part. *(Beat.)* It's all well and good that you think Kelly is the right person for the part. But this is her first play. She didn't earn it. And I did. I can do it! And . . . the worst part of all is that you gave me the old woman part. I am not an old woman. Can't I for once play the girl who gets the guy? Why am I being punished? It's just not fair. And if I don't get the right part, the fair part, I'm going to quit. *(Beat.)* I'm sorry, but that's how it is.

THE BIG SULK

CLAIRE

Congratulations, Mike. You deserve it. The best person won, I guess.

Mom and Dad, can we just go home now? *(Beat.)* Because . . . I'm trying really hard to be big about this, but I'm really upset. And I don't want anyone to see it. *(Beat.)* I deserved that award. I worked hard all year. I just don't kiss the teacher's butt. I know it sounds like sour grapes, but I really think it's true. My science fair project was way more labor-intensive and difficult. His was easy. He never takes chances. *(Beat.)* I participate in class! I've busted my ass all year and what do I get for it? Nothing. What a complete waste. Good-bye scholarship. Good-bye decent college. All because I couldn't be a kiss up like that moron. *(Beat.)* Listen, you can just stand here and chat with the other parents, but I'm getting out of here. I'll be in the car.

Male Monologues

• • •

COMEDY

DOESN'T ADD UP

GUS

My life is ruined. 900. That is my combined score. 900. Out of 1600. That's seven hundred points short of a perfect score. Or is it? Because I clearly can't do math. So maybe I'm wrong. Why do I even go to school? It's doing no good. And I'll never get into college now. I should just give up and get work in a factory. I'm not good for anything else. I'll find myself a nice, little wife who strips three nights a week when she's not looking after our five children because we're too dumb to bother with birth control. Of course, she's had an affair with my brother, but I still love her. She's the mother of our children.

Listen, I gotta go. I never paid attention in wood shop and never took auto mechanics. I think Mr. Messler and I have a lot to talk about regarding my future. It was nice seeing you. At our ten-year reunion, we'll compare beer guts. Boy, we had some good times.

HAIRY PROBLEMS

WOLF

That thing people say about women not liking hairy backs? True. That stuff about Teen Wolf being popular? False. Pure Hollywood fluff. When puberty descends on you so fast, you start to wonder where it will stop. I am a teen nightmare! I practically bathe in deodorant. Gym class is a nightmare.

How can you tell your mom you want to get your back waxed? Believe me, there's no way. First of all, it's totally embarrassing. Second of all, I actually tried and she just told me I was adorable. When will they understand that statements like that don't actually help?

Summer is coming up. I'm preparing for total hibernation. The beach is not possible, man. No way. Not in this lifetime.

TWENTY-FIRST CENTURY

ADAM

This is beyond cruel. Why does this responsibility fall to us? Everyone talks about how it's the twenty-first century and all that, but girls never ask us out. At least they never ask guys like us out. Maybe the football captains . . . No, not even them. But at least they know that girls will say yes when they ask. We don't have any assurances like that. We just have to trust the girl's friend's friend or their little sister or their second cousin that the girl actually maybe likes us. And pray it's not some kind of practical joke. Or that we don't say anything stupid and scare her off. Or that her friend's friend's cousin doesn't tell her the football captain wants to ask her out, in which case, she'll never say yes to me.

Oh, hi, Isabelle. Uh, uh, uh . . . yeah. Sure. That sounds swell.

Did I just say swell? Wait — I think I have a date! I have a date!

BUDDY BOY

MATT

I gotta say this. Don't take this the wrong way, but it kinda bugs me how girls feel like they can talk to me about anything. Their cramps. Their body issues. It's not fair. I like talking to you and listening to you and hanging out with you, but there need to be limits. Homosexuals and artists and freaks and nerds are not *girls*. We are *guys* who understand you a little better. But, but we're still *male*. I'm still human. Mostly. I'm not your cat or your diary. Tell me about stuff that goes on with you — I want you to — but leave out the really serious girl stuff. Please?

If I hear one more complaint about your PMS, I'm sorry, but I'm going to have a huge hissy fit.

BAD TIMING

EVAN

I've been wanting to talk to you about something. We've been friends for a long time. We get along so well. We like the same things. It's just that . . . I've been thinking . . . *You're* not dating anyone and *I'm* not dating anyone . . .

What? Colin? But — that's great, I guess, but do you have anything in common with him? Picture it. You're on a date somewhere, getting a bite to eat. You have to come up with something to talk about. All Colin talks about is sports and his hair. Whether he looks better with his hair parted to the right or the left. Yeah, maybe the left is better, but . . .

Oh, never mind.

BAD TO THE EPIDERMIS

SEAN

I'm just too nice. No one likes a nice guy. I try to be bad, to be a rebel. It never quite works. I stole a book from Barnes and Noble. Know what happened? My mother found it, read it and said it changed her life. For the better. She *thanked* me. *(Beat.)* I don't know. Some Dr. Phil book.

Then I told Jim Raymond he could bite me. So what does he do? He bites me. So hard. *(Beat.)* Yeah, I cried. So would you. But I stood up to him; told him what I thought of him. How come no one's flirting with me, exposing her navel and twisting her hair around her finger in my presence? I tell you, women are a mystery.

I bought this leather jacket. *(Beat.)* Yeah, it is cool, isn't it? But know what Lina said to me? She said I looked cute. I said, "Cute?" thinking maybe this was a good thing. Then she goes, "Yeah, sweet. Like you're wearing your dad's clothes." I was like, "Excuse me?" Can you believe it? I give up. Are there still monasteries? Do you need to be religious to join one?

GEEK GOD

BEN

I've been working out. Joined a gym over the summer. Check out my biceps. Thought I might go out for the wrestling team this year. *(Beat.)* What's the problem?

I know jocks have always been the enemy. So I thought, fight fire with fire. They're no better than us. And I'm gonna prove it. Why not beat them at their own game? Listen, I learned a lot about working out, my mom got me a private trainer; I could help you, too.

I'm not saying you need to be ashamed of yourself. I mean, you're fine. I just thought — *(Beat.)* Man, you are taking this all wrong. This is not a betrayal. I'm just thinking, if we've got brains *and* brawn, we could take over this school. Just imagine . . . our group on the student council, being the jocks, dating the hottest girls. We could rule the world! Once we take over the key strongholds commonly held by the cool and the popular, we could force our taste on the entire school. Everyone will be dying to take up chess and work the video equipment.

Let's start with push-ups. Give me twenty now!

YOU WISH

PAUL

I'm going away to college, as far from here as I can get. California. Land of sunshine and movie stars. Land of tans that don't come in bottles and blondes that do. Everywhere you look — bikinis! Flesh. Toned and surgically altered flesh. Perfection everywhere the eye can see. *(Beat.)* Shut up! I will too fit in. What are you looking at? Strippers are going to drink pink cocktails off of this stomach. *(Beat.)* What movies have I been watching? Documentaries. In fact, I'll make a documentary of my first year of college and mail it to you. Try not to cry too much.

So, enjoy the cold winters and the wooly sweaters of home. See ya, bud, wouldn't want to be ya.

WISH YOU WERE HERE

MIKE

Oh my God, you don't have a shirt on. Oh, you don't speak English. And I don't speak French. And . . . oh my God, you don't have a shirt on. Okay, be cool. Be cool. I'm going to look in your eyes. You have lovely eyes. Brown. And whatever I do, I am not going to look —

I'm sorry. I'm sorry. It's just that . . . you don't have a shirt on. And I am a red-blooded teenager. You can't just walk around like that and not have people, such as myself, looking at . . . you. It's impossible. I'm trying. Honestly.

Are you laughing at me?

Oh my God. You *do* speak English. So . . . sorry. Really. I've just never seen anyone just walk around like that! And . . . and . . . oh my God, you don't have a top on!

UNDER THE BLEACHERS

MORGAN

You're beautiful. I mean it. You are H-O-T hot. *(Beat.)* I don't mean to embarrass you. It's just that I've been staring at the back of your head in math class all year and it's the last day of school and my family's moving . . . So, you see, I've got nothing to lose. So . . . here goes. I like you. You're smart and funny and cute. You've got great hair and I should know. I may not be the most popular person, but I'm fun.

Hellooooo. Cat got your tongue? You there? *(Beat.)* This is hard for me. Don't think I do this every day. Listen, here's the deal. Think it over. And meet me under the bleachers in five minutes. *(Beat.)* Don't be stupid. This is the best offer you'll get all year.

DEALING WITH LOSS

WILL

Can you keep a secret? Okay. This must be a secret. I think . . .
I think I'm losing my hair. There just seems to be more on my
brush than before. And the shower drain gets all clogged. Yeah,
I'm know it's gross. *(Beat.)* Don't you see? I'll never be — you
know. Loved.

Shut up! This is serious. Prom is coming up. What if I'm bald
by then? Dude, my chances are already slim of getting a good
date. Now I'm in serious jeopardy. And college? Forget about
it. No fraternity will want me. I'll go right from being sixteen
to forty, thinking about rules and how many miles per gallon
my car gets . . .

What do you mean, shave it? *(Beat.)* I owe you about a mil-
lion! Wait — what if my head is misshapen? Where are you
going?

HOLLYWOOD, HERE I COME

MILES

Excuse me; we're filming here. If you absolutely must walk in front of our cameras, could you at least pretend you're zombies? Please, I may be a kid, but so were all the famous directors. We all have to start somewhere. Please, please, will anyone listen to me? I just need you not to walk in this little tiny area here while we film for, like, ten minutes. This is not too much to ask! Please, stop! Just walk around us. Please!

This is my fourth film. I am not an amateur! I demand respect!

Okay. Actors — places. We're all clear. And . . . action! Yes, you walk in, zombie-like, and —

Oh my lord! I'm ruined. Ruined! You people are killing me. I'm only seventeen and I am now having a heart attack and my ulcer is bleeding! Just know that the next brilliant Fellini, the next Tarantino, the next freakin' Coppola is dying on the sidewalk just because you clowns can't keep from walking on this tiny bit of sidewalk for five minutes.

Oh, sure. *Now* you stand still and stare like zombies. Why couldn't you do that when we were filming!

BOULDER ROCKS

BOULDER

Why can't I be a rock star? *(Beat.)* Just because I'm fat? So what? I'm talented. I can rock harder than anyone I know. I can actually play instruments. Girls like me, too. *(Beat.)* Okay, maybe they don't want to jump my bones — yet — but I'm hopeful on that score.

I love to make trouble. I go to public pools and do huge cannonballs. People get so crazy mad at me! Not to mention my shoplifting. I stole a packet of ballpoint pens just last week. In PE just this week, when Pendleton told me to move my fat haunches, I told him, "Make me." Just like that, all dangerous. "Make me."

I've got a demo; I never get sick on the bus. I could tour for years. Give me a break, man.

What gives you the right to judge me anyhow? Just because you're a judge at this contest? Take a good look, buddy. People will be paying millions someday to watch this fat ass exit a room.

DREAM (ALMOST) COME TRUE

JEREMY

Ladies, Ladies. You're embarrassing yourselves. There's enough of me to go around. Whoa, watch the hands! I know, I know. I'm a world-famous rock star and irresistible to boot, but if you take your turn . . . Okay, okay. Two at a time. But no more. I am human, after all. I am! I know it's hard to believe —

Hi. There. Daphne. I didn't see you there. How long were you — Wait. Don't answer that. Would you believe that I'm . . . rehearsing for a play. *(Beat.)* That's right. I have the lead. He's a rock star —

Hey, you're . . . touching me. You think I'd be a great rock star? Well, I do play the trumpet in the school band. Third chair.

Actually, I'm really ticklish. Could you not touch me th —

Wait! Where are you going? I'm a rock star; remember! Wait!

CHILLING

HUGH

Yeah, hi. *(Beat.)* Yeah, I'm that guy. *(Beat.)* I'm glad you liked the film. Yeah, it was great working with Steve; he's a great director. *(Beat.)* Sorry to interrupt, but I'm having dinner with my friends here. *(Beat.)* No, don't get all upset. Don't cry. Oh God. Please, take it easy. It really is great meeting you. It's great to meet my fans. I wouldn't be anything without you, right? But can you understand that sometimes I want to just hang out with my friends? Just like you do with your friends, I'm sure.

It's nothing against you. I mean it. You're great. Just look at you. You're . . . a great person. *(Beat.)* Yeah, I mean it. You're very sweet. *(Beat.)* Of course I'll sign an autograph, just don't cry, okay? *(Beat.)* Um, no. I can't go meet your friends. I'm *eating*. *(Beat.)* Don't cry. Oh, God.

ESCAPE

HARRY

I, Harry Houdini, will escape from these ropes and chains be... your very eyes!

(Struggling.)

Behold, magic is about to happen! Prepare to be amazed!

(Struggling.)

Mom, help! I'm in my room! I know I said I wouldn't do this again, but I did.

Honest, Mom, I need help! If you want to teach me a lesson, there are lots of other ways to do it. You could ground me . . . or take away my ropes for a week. Come on! I have to go to the bathroom!

Can anyone hear me? Fire! The room is on fire! *(Beat.)* Oh, come on. I'm really uncomfortable here. I promise I'll never do this again!

TRICK OR TEEN

TOM

I'm a teenager. Yep. Pretty good costume, right? Very realistic. I think it's treat time. *(Beat.)* Come on. I am not too old. I'm a growing boy. I need candy. I made the effort to walk all the way over here, in costume, just like all these little kids. Why shouldn't I get a treat?

Okay, okay! I live next door. You got me there. But it's one piece of candy. Don't be a miser.

Thanks. Listen. You've got a lot of candy there and my favorite is actually the Crunch bar. I'm bigger than those other kids. I need more nourishment. Can't you bend your rules just this once?

The "whole damn thing" if I just go away? You bet. Gee, thanks, Mrs. Jenner! See you next year!

FUNNY GUY

JACK

You smell like poo, man. I'm not kidding. *(Beat.)* I would not say that as a joke. Where have you been? Not to get personal, but did you wipe? Honest to God, man to man, you stink. *(Beat.)* Yeah, go check it out. Please.

I can't believe he believed us. What a dink.

I do not smell. *(Beat.)* No, man, I made that up. You can't fool me at my own game. *(Beat.)* No! Quit it. Dude, I haven't even done number two today. And I did not deal one. Maybe you did, man.

Shut up! Oh, whatever. I'm out of here. *(Beat.)* Where am I going? That's none of your business.

By the way, you stink, man. I'm serious.

VLAD TO THE BONE

DRACULA

Come to me. *(Beat.)* Yes, you. I said, "Come to me!" in a creepy, commanding tone. *(Beat.)* What do you mean why? Because I told you to. I have possession of your soul. Look deep into my eyes. You are imprisoned by me. You cannot look away. *(Beat.)* I said, "You cannot look away." That guy is not hot. That is my servant. He eats bugs. Surely you cannot be imprisoned by this sorry creature of the night. It defies logic. *(Beat.)* I do not use too much gel. I am debonair.

This look is timeless. Ageless. Like me. I don't need to don the attire of your time. *(Beat.)* "It would help?" How dare you speak so to me! No, I don't drive. I fly. Oh, I give up. *(Beat.)* Do you think I have a shot with that girl over there? The shorter one with the pink shirt. *(Beat.)* No? Don't tempt me to take your soul. I could, if I wanted to.

TAKING CONTROL

JUDE

Come here. Come on. Closer. Listen, you need to know something. You make me crazy. Like I'm going to explode. I've been trying to hold back, but I can't wait any longer. You're fantastic. You're cute. I like you. Really like you. You know what I'm trying to say to you?

How about you come over to my house this weekend? My parents are away. We could rent a movie, or not. Whatever you want. Whatever it takes. So, do you like me, Denise? I'm okay, right?

I'm gonna be so good to you. I swear. Come with me to McDonald's. It's on me. You can even super-size your meal. I'm loaded. Here's five bucks. There's lots more where that came from.

EXCUSE MY FRENCH

JJ

Je ne understand pas. *(Beat.)* What? I can't understand you. *(Beat.)* Okay. Je ne . . . *comprends* pas. I don't understand. *(Beat.)* Nope, still don't get it. *(Beat.)* Nope. Do you think . . . maybe you could speak in English? Just for a second? *(Beat.)* Je *still* don't comprends pas. I cannot understand anything you are saying. *(Beat.)* I *know* this is French class. Thank you for saying that in English, by the way. *(Beat.)* I *know* you speak French in French class but what you need to know is that I am a *transfer* student who can't speak French. So even though this is a beginning French class, everyone else has been in this class for two months already and I really can't understand you.

I'm not bluffing. You'll have to say it in English. *(Beat.)* Oh, they told me I *had* to take a foreign language class. *(Beat.)* I had French class in my old school; they just spoke in English mostly and we repeated after the teacher. Like the teacher would say, "Bonjour!" And we'd say, "Bonjour!" Like that.

What else do I know? Voilà! Uh, monsieur, madame, escargot, Gerard Depardieu — I think that's it.

RESTFUL/RESTLESS

RYAN

I can't sleep anymore. It's really depressing. I thought if I kept staying up at some point my body would take over and I'd just conk out. But it hasn't happened for two weeks.

No way am I going to exercise. I'd rather die. Do you really think it matters? *(Beat.)* I mean, I walk up and down the stairs at home a couple of times a day when I need to get a snack. Otherwise, I stay in my room, listen to music, watch TV. It's summer break. Isn't that what we're supposed to do?

So, you sleep don't you? *(Beat.)* This is killing me. I even tried reading last night to try to get to sleep. *(Beat.)* It was some crappy book about, I don't know, kings or something.

Could you pass me the remote? I don't wanna get up.

SMALL TOWN BLUES

REGGIE

Are there any nightclubs in this town? *(Beat.)* Where do you shop? *(Beat.)* At the Gap? Seriously? This is like *Happy Days*. What do you do here for fun?

You drive around and yell at people out of the windows. Do you go to parties? *(Beat.)* Okay, let me see if I've got this straight. You drive with no destination whatsoever so you can attract the attention of people you don't know. Okay.

How about tipping over cows or knocking mailboxes down or spray-painting the school? *(Beat.)* Are you sure? Because I've seen that in movies. You're really scaring me now. Please tell me that dancing is not against the law. I haven't wandered into some pre-*Footloose* dimension, have I?

Oh, thank God. So, what do you say we shake things up around here? Point me to the nearest cow.

SHUT UP, EVERYONE

CAMERON

I can't sleep at night. It's too loud! Does everyone have a car alarm? How is it possible? No one seems to even own a car. Where are all these cars coming from? And why does everyone think I want to listen to their music? If I wanted to listen to salsa music at midnight, I'd play it myself!

And the light! Don't get me started on the lights. Car lights, streetlights, the hall lights in our apartment are on all night . . .

Where we used to live, all you could hear at night would be crickets, the wind blowing. And it was dark. Like it's supposed to be. Isn't darkness part of the definition of night?

All these damn kids walking around the streets, yelling and playing after ten P.M. — Don't they have parents? Isn't there a curfew?

Whoa. I'm in big trouble now. I sound like a parent! I've gone completely mad from lack of sleep. *(Beat.)* I don't even know who you are! Why am I talking to you? Help! I'm talking to strangers!

SIMON'S SECRET

SIMON

Mom, don't come in my room. I'm busy. Don't! Excuse you.

I have no idea where Mary's magazines are. Why would I know that? Mom, I am a guy. I have no interest in Victoria Secret catalogs. Or . . . whatever she claims to have lost.

Get away from my bed! That is my territory. *(Beat.)* No, I have nothing to hide. I just don't want you in my stuff. What's going on here? How come you're so fascist lately? Who cares about a bunch of dumb magazines anyway? What's so important about women's underwear anyway? It's just a bunch of chicks sitting on sofas in bras and panties and thongs — so what? Not that I've ever seen it. I'm just guessing.

Listen, if I happen to see any of Mary's magazines anywhere, I'll return them to her. Meanwhile, can I get a little privacy here?

CURSED

DYLAN

No! No. I didn't say . . . *that*. I said pluck. Referring, of course, to the sassiness of my dear sister here. Boy, does she have pluck. I'll be plucked if she isn't plucky!

I was not cursing! Honestly. You know, when you get older, your hearing starts to go. No offense, but maybe it's started, Dad. Maybe this is the first sign of the years taking their toll. You must be — what? — fifty-five? *(Beat.)* Forty-eight. That's what I meant. Forty-eight.

Okay, I'm sorry. I didn't mean to do it. It just slipped out. So, give me a break. *(Beat.)* Like you never say any curse words. You say them all the time, then you tell me I can't. That's hypocritical. *(Beat.)* No! It isn't a privilege of being an adult. I'm not some stupid little kid, Dad. If you can say it, so can I. And if you don't like it, well, *pluck you!*

BIG TALK

TIO

I am fearless! I will absolutely kick everyone else's ass in this competition. I am stronger, smarter, faster, and braver than anyone here. I can hold my breath for three minutes. I love heights. Snakes, alligators — bring it on! I'm lovin' this!

What is that? *(Beat.)* You want me to . . . eat that? That is the nastiest thing I've ever seen. *(Beat.)* Chew it? *All* of it? *(Beat.)* No problem! You guys are going down!

Yep, I'm ready. Here I go. Chowing on bloody, squishy insects. Looks good. I'm psyched, man! *(Beat.)* Okay, only ten seconds left. No sweat. I'm gonna love this. I can't wait to sink my teeth into this. I'm gonna chomp on those live bugs like they were pizza! You are —

Time's up? But I was going to win! I was going to suck down those creepy, crawly —

Excuse me. I'm gonna be sick!

THIRTY-TWO FLAVORS

JOE

Listen, that's your sixth sample. Can't you just pick a flavor and go with it? You're making my life really difficult. You're an adult and I'm just a kid. You weigh, like, twice what I do. No offense or anything. *(Beat.)* My point is, we both know you've got the power here. But do you have to be such a pig? I'm just trying to make my lousy minimum wage; I really don't need any trouble. Can't you just go with, say, the Rocky Road? You seemed to like that.

My boss is going to totally yell at me. I'm not supposed to give more than two samples. *(Beat.)* Buddy, look, I'm begging you. I'll sneak you an extra scoop. Just pick!

Oh God, a family just came in. Can you understand the importance of this? There's no time to waste, man! Pick! For God's sake, pick!

CAR TROUBLE

ARI

Okay, go, go, go! I can't parallel park so get out now! God, they're beeping already. Hurry! I want a poppy seed bagel with cream cheese and a Coke! *Did you hear me?*

I'm sorry, dude. I'll get out of the way soon. *(Beat.)* There's plenty of room. Drive around me! *(Beat.)* Geez, go over the dotted line. There's no one else here. I won't tell. Just do it! *(Beat.)* Listen, I can't move. You don't understand. I cannot parallel park. I am doing my best and you are making me hella nervous, so stop it!

Chill! Fine! I'll move, I'll move!

Oh God! Look what you made me do, you idiot! I hit that car and it's all your fault! *(Beat.)* Oh, *now* you're driving away. Great.

Thank God. Get in. Quick! We gotta motor!

DISSECT THIS

AARON

Ready? Three, two, one — throw!

That is so satisfying. Nothing is more gratifying than hearing forty girls screaming their heads off. What's so scary about a hollowed-out, dissected frog anyway? Sure, they smell bad, formaldehyde and all, but if you ask me, the frog is *less* disgusting once the insides are gone.

The best part of it is the way the bus just drives away and we basically get off scot-free, isn't it? Such a rush.

Oh, hi, Mrs. Bishop. *(Beat.)* No, we were just discussing our science homework, that's all.

TO HAVE OR TO HAVE NOT

RIPLEY

We need cable. I mean it. I am the only person on the face of the Earth who doesn't have it. *(Beat.)* Ha-ha. Fine. Besides you and maybe a couple of people over eighty. But everybody else has it. *(Beat.)* Uh — you are so difficult! Fine, so people in the Third World don't have it. Enough already! You know what I'm saying.

Listen. Kids talk about TV. It gives us stuff in common to talk about. The way adults talk about bills and jobs and what pains their kids are. You are keeping me from connecting with my age group. Making me an outsider. Giving me a complex and reducing my self-esteem. Isn't having a healthy kid who has friends worth forty bucks a month?

KINGS AND PEONS

PALMER

Here we are, at the threshold of our future. Graduating at last. So what does the future hold?

Some will lead "normal" lives, populating the planet and working at banks. You people are on your own. I really have nothing to say to you. Your place in the universe is clear and extremely depressing.

The elite will influence future generations to come. Those people will write for television sitcoms. I'd like to speak for a moment to those future leaders. Please, let's not encourage people to be friends and interface in coffee shops. Don't tell stories about wacky teens kidnapping the rival school's mascot. Nobody does that. Do schools even use livestock as mascots anymore? No. It's just some nerd in an enormous animal head. Try to be original. Don't do a remake of some half-baked show from the eighties. No one wants to see *90210* in the year 2020. For one thing, Luke Perry will be eighty-seven by then.

Now go out and boldly be either revolutionary or entirely ordinary. The class of 2005 rules!

Male Monologues

• • •

DRAMA

BETWEEN

STEPHEN

No, I'm not going to Mom's. *(Beat.)* So what I'm supposed to, it's her weekend. It's my weekend, too, and I'm not going. *(Beat.)* Listen, it's just way more fun here. And there's this girl at the video store who's cool. You let us eat pizza for breakfast. Dad, you're cool. And Mom's not. We see her almost all the time.

Can't I stay? *(Beat.)* Why? *(Beat.)* Don't you care about me? How come you don't like me? Why don't you just come out and say you don't care? Why do we come here at all? It's just a stupid pretence.

You're a joke, by the way. Always trying to be cool. You're not. You're old. And boring. And embarrassing. At least Mom knows she's a mom. *(Beat.)* Just leave me alone unless you decide you really want me around.

PUSHING IT

DANNY

Listen, you can't keep me here. We both know it. So why bother grounding me? It's a joke. *(Beat.)* I can't take you seriously when you go all parent-y on me. You can put your foot down all you want. Nothing you do can make me follow your rules. I'm bigger than you. I'm at least as smart as you. *(Beat.)* You're not going to throw me out on the street; I'm your kid.

So, let's approach this from an adult perspective, okay? *(Beat.)* I'll tell you what that means. I want to go out tonight. You don't want me to. What if I go out tonight and — here's the part you'll like — get back by eleven? And to sweeten the deal for me, you'll give me fifty bucks in exchange for my curfew. *(Beat.)* No, that's the deal. Otherwise, I'll just go out and come back whenever I like.

Go ahead. Kick me out of the house. As if.

CONFESSION

TOBY

It made sense. Go in the house. Steal the money. Any ATM cards, credit cards. When that lady came in the room, well, it . . . I got panicked. You know? So I just grabbed what was at hand. I didn't really think about it. I just hit her with this gavel thing, like lawyers have. She started screaming so I had to hit her a lot. Over and over again. I just kept thinking, "Shut up! Shut up or someone's going to come!"

I was obsessed in that moment with just getting out, getting away without . . . without getting in trouble. It's almost funny. Without getting in trouble. I'm in the worst trouble ever. The worst trouble anyone can be in. I threw my life away. I ruined my life. It's not fair.

LOCKED AND LOADED

EMERSON

I don't know why everyone is so upset about guns. You just have to know how to use them. A smart person should be able to have one. Why not? For hunting or protecting yourself. You never know what psycho might show up at your door. You have to be prepared.

It's no different, really, than the idea that rock music makes you a Satanist. If you have a brain, even if you're listening to some band saying something about killing or whatever, you're not going to do it. No singer can make me a murderer and having a gun doesn't make me a killer.

SCARS

DAZ

My brother was done in. At McDonald's. There's no way I can get through this world without scars. I'm sixteen already. I got this one on my forehead when I was ten. This one on my arm, that was a knife a few weeks back.

I gotta put some cocoa butter on it so the skin doesn't get hard. If you don't, your skin kinda pulls and it hurts. I made that mistake a while back and I got one that aches bad.

But it's all bullshit. I see that. It's crazy that I gotta think about watching my back every minute in addition to doing my homework. As if history class wasn't hard enough. There's some kind of — what do you call it? — irony about not being able to learn history and us kids setting out to keep knifing each other day after day. Don't make sense.

HELPLESS

MEL

Grandpa, can you hear me? Your eyes look like you can hear me. It must be pretty awful in there. I don't mean to depress you or anything. I just can't help thinking this must be the worst thing in the world. Having your mind work but your body doesn't. There must be loads of things you want to say and do. To be honest, I'm really scared of getting old. Not just getting sick, although that is bad, but also just having stuff give out on you. Like this guy I see getting on the bus in the morning. It takes him ages just to climb the steps to get on.

I wish I knew what I could say to make it better for you. I don't know. I guess I just want you to know that I see that you hear me and all that.

REGRETS

GREG

What's worse: saying something bad to someone or not saying something you really want to say? I think I regret more the things I didn't say. *(Beat.)* Here it is, summertime, and I never told Dana Winkler from my bio class how much I really, really liked her. What's the worst that could have happened? She would have laughed at me. Mocked me. So what. I've withstood taunting before. I could have told people she was lying. Why am I such a wimp?

Everyone is so scared of doing something that's socially wrong. Of being different or calling attention to themselves. We're all so busy trying to be like everyone else that we don't even know who we are or what we like anymore. No one is an individual anymore. Why are we all so nuts? Does this ever go away or are we destined to be insecure maniacs forever? That's something to look forward to.

WANTING AND WAITING

EMMETT

Pete, I think something's seriously wrong with me. Tell me if you think I'm mental. *(Beat.)* Okay. I'm all messed up. I mean, I can't concentrate. My thinking is all off. I can't manage to do anything I'm supposed to. I'm kind of in pain and anxious all the time. There's a tightness in my chest and my stomach is freaking out . . .

Well, there's this girl. And I can't stop thinking about her. And I'm really trying! I have loads to do, exams coming up and all. So, I'm becoming, like, obsessed or something. *(Beat.)* I saw her in the grocery store the other day and I really, seriously considered following her home. I managed to stop myself, but I've been to that grocery store four times since to see if she'd come back.

Honestly, I'm really worried that I've gone over the edge. Your parents are psychiatrists, so I thought maybe you had some idea about this kind of thing, that maybe they talked about stuff . . . What's wrong with me?

GOOD ENOUGH

BUCK

Yeah, it's no big. She ignores me when other people are around, but when we're alone . . . *(Beat.)* Yeah, she's wild. So, it's worth it. Really. I don't mind. *(Beat.)* Nah, we don't do any of those "date" things. We just hang out. In private.

Lay off, man. She is not ashamed of me . . . exactly. And so what if she is? All my friends know I have a girlfriend and I know I have a girlfriend and that's cool.

Okay, fine, it sucks. But what am I supposed to do? Isn't it better to have a girlfriend who pretends you're invisible better than not having a girlfriend at all? I get to make out with a girl who's kinda popular and pretty and cool and all I have to do is not talk to her in school. It's a trade-off. That's what life's about — compromise.

How long will it go on? I guess until she decides she can do better than me. Who knows? Maybe I'll find someone else. You never know.

PATIENT

DAMON

I get it. I understand that this is a big deal, especially for girls. But here's the thing. Is there ever going to be a really perfect time? You could wait forever for that. So why not now? You know I care about you. You definitely know I want you. *(Beat.)* Believe me, I won't dump you afterwards.

I'm going to say something potentially awful sounding here. I don't mean it that way; I'm just being practical. If a guy has any chance of getting sex more than once with a girl, why would he leave? Unless he was absolutely guaranteed that another girl would do it with him, you're going to go with the sure thing, right?

I am not being a jerk. I knew you'd take it like that. I am just trying to talk this out. That's what you wanted, didn't you? I personally think it's a waste of time. *(Beat.)* We've had this conversation a hundred times! I just don't want to have it anymore. I think *you* should be honest with *me* now. Is there any chance that we will actually get past this phase and actually do it? Or is this it? *(Beat.)* Well, this isn't enough. And it's getting really boring.

SECURE

BRYAN

I don't know why. I'm just confident. Why not? *(Beat.)* There's
no secret. I just wake up in the morning and don't think much
at all. "Hey, that's me in the mirror." "It's Wednesday, right?"
Those are the things I think. Nothing deep. I guess I just know
nothing's going to be that bad. People like me for the most part.
I'm not incredible at anything, not bad at anything. Everything
works out more or less. Okay at sports. Not the last picked for
the team or anything. I just don't let things get to me. *(Beat.)*
You ought to try it sometime. Don't analyze and think so much.
It's overrated. Just let stuff happen. Whatever.

Look, it's actually hard to be around you when you analyze stuff
all the time. You're kind of a downer. You're all glass half empty.
(Beat.) So, yeah. I'm actually gonna go.

WORKING IT OUT

MAX

You make me so mad; you know that? I don't know what it is about you. Why do you always bring me down whenever I'm happy? All my dreams are impractical. I should be rational. I ought to work harder. Why can't you just give me unconditional support? You're my father — would it be so hard? It's your job. Can't you just say, "You got a B plus in your hardest subject; that's great!" instead of "You'll do better next time"?

I know you're trying to be nice. That's the worst part. You're always trying to be helpful, so I look like a jerk when I get mad. *(Beat.)* When I'm sad, don't say, "Just keep trying. Maybe if you work harder, things will improve." What I want to hear is "I'm so sorry. Everything will be okay." Even if it's a lie. Just some sympathy. I don't always want to *work* to be better. Maybe I can't get any better. Maybe I'm tired of working.

You're not a bad father. And I definitely don't think you should work harder at it. Take it easy for once.

SECOND BEST

GRAY

You never show up to any of my plays, Dad. And you always go to Jordy's games. *(Beat.)* I know you like sports and you respect football more than theater, but it would mean a lot to me . . . I just feel like you don't care about me, Dad.

This is important to me. So are you and Mom. When you look down on what I do . . . It's just not fair. Jordy's not a better person. He never even tries at anything. He's just lucky. Always lucky. Not only is he great at sports and all the girls like him and the guys respect him, he's your favorite. Just because he got the good genes. Would it kill you to just give me a little attention and respect sometimes?

OUT

LOUIS

So, I just told my dad. He was totally silent. At least he didn't hit me or anything. Yet. Or maybe that would be better. He's a marine, that's his way. I just know he's never going to accept me now. It's bad enough that he never liked me.

I think he's always suspected I'm gay. I just can't stand pretending anymore. Do you think my mom will stop accepting me, too, now? She was okay about it before. She says she loves me anyway. Maybe she'll leave my dad and we'll live together, the two of us. Can I be totally honest with you? *(Beat.)* That's actually what I've always wanted.

My dad is never going to like me or who I am. What I am. God, you'd think me telling him the truth would show him that I'm a strong person. Brave even. It was hard saying anything to him. The hardest thing I've ever done.

I wish he would have said something. He just walked away. Stared and walked away. *(Beat.)* Straight people never have to come out and tell their parents who they'd like to have sex with someday. How come we do? It isn't right. I just hope my life doesn't get even worse now.

THE DECISION

BRAD

Jesus doesn't want us to be gay. The church says it's not right. So I'm not going to be. *(Beat.)* It *is* something I can just decide. I don't know why I ever felt any other way.

My parents always told me I can be anything I want to be. And I want to be heterosexual. So I am. I never really was anything else. I've never done it with anyone. So forget what I said before. I was confused. Stupid. *(Beat.)* If you tell anyone, I'll say you're a liar. And I'll tell them what you are.

Come on. I don't want us to be enemies. You are the only person who listened to me, talked to me, when . . . you know, I was going through stuff. I just thought maybe we could help each other. Start a new life. *(Beat.)* I do believe in God and I want to be a better person. It's not being dishonest. It's wanting a better life. An easier life. And I do want a family and kids. Don't you?

That's what you want to hear; what you want to believe. It's not true. There aren't ways to find love and have a family and be a homosexual. Society won't accept you. And I'm not strong enough for that. *(Beat.)* I'm sorry if I'm disappointing you, but that's how I feel.

STREET TALK

HAWK

My parents kicked me out. I told them my uncle abused me. And it was the truth. They told me I was a liar. I wasn't an angel, I'll admit. I'm not the best kid in the world. But that was the truth.

I'm glad they kicked me out, though. Now I don't ever have to see my uncle again or be around people who have no respect for me. Who don't trust or believe me when I really need them to.

We look out for each other here. We're like a community. Everyone has a story. A lot have a story like mine. Or drugs. Or they're gay. Or all of the above. The hardest part is the obvious stuff. Food, drink, shelter. It gets really cold in the winter. There are times you want to give up, you just want to die, but no one will let you. We're real friends. Not the phony kind you have when you're a kid. "I'll be your best friend if you let me have your video game." You don't have to bribe anyone.

Unless you get into the drug thing. And I won't lie. It's hard not to. Forgetting can be a really good thing. But then you end up in a whole sex spiral trying to get money for your next fix. Stick with me. You'll be okay.

ON THE LINE

CALVIN

Don't hang up. Please, don't. I want to help you. Tell me what's wrong. Sometimes it just helps to say it. *(Beat.)* Maybe I won't understand. But try me. I've heard just about everything. Probably worse things than you're going through. You wouldn't believe the things people can live through. *(Beat.)* What if I told you something I'm dealing with? Last week a girl called and killed herself while she was talking to me. It was the worst thing I've ever had to deal with. Please don't make me go through it again. *(Beat.)* I know it's not my fault, but I feel guilty. Thinking about what I could have said or done. I have to live with this girl's death forever. Please. Tell me anything. Tell me you've been beaten or raped or cut from the cheerleading team — anything. Just talk to me. We can work this out. I really want to try to help. Trust me when I tell you that your death will screw up a lot more people than just you.

MEANING OF LIFE

ANDREW

What is the point of my whole life? I'm destined to be alone, so it's not to have a family and all that. I won't be the scientist who's going to cure cancer. It's not to accomplish anything because I am useless. I have nothing to add to this world. No one's ever gone out of their way to tell me I'm good at anything. No one even particularly likes me. People put up with me. People just put up with me. Where does this leave me? Why was I born?

I'm not depressed. I don't need help. I'm not crazy. I'm just a failure, that's all.

FEAR

PHOENIX

I can't stand watching the news anymore. Can we change the channel? *(Beat.)* I know it's important to know about your world, but when I see all this stuff about Iraq and Israel and all those places, I can't help thinking about the kids that live there. Kids my age. I know what it's like to be scared of something happening to you. And it must be even worse for them. But we never see that. So it makes me sad and mad to see this stuff on TV. It's always so one-sided. If people could think more about who they are destroying, kids like me, kids with parents like them, maybe the world wouldn't have so many problems.

When you really think about the reality of what it's like to die from a bomb, for instance, it's horrible. Maybe your skin will be burned off your body. You could be psychologically scarred for the rest of your life by what you've seen. I don't mean to be graphic, but we really ought to think of things like that.

If you wouldn't want that kind of fate for you or your kids, why would you want that for other people? *(Beat.)* I'm not saying it's right for people to do evil things. I'm saying the opposite. But it just seems to me that if people thought about consequences more and who they are hurting besides dictators and all that, maybe the world would be a better place. You just shouldn't have to be scared all the time, no matter where in the world you live, when you're only a teenager.

UNNATURAL DISASTER

JOHN

My life is ruined. I've lost everything. Every word I ever wrote is gone. There's no way I can make up all the work lost on my computer. *(Beat.)* I know I should have backed it up on disks — at least I know it now — but don't tell me that. That's not what I need to hear. It does me no good. It just makes me miserable. Like when you tell me to be careful after I hurt myself. It does no good and I'm already miserable enough. Why do you want to add to it and torture me? *(Beat.)* I swear; you hate me. Just dump me off in a field somewhere to be picked apart by vultures. It'll be better than going to school tomorrow.

NO FRIEND OF MINE

TONY

You want me to feel sorry for you, but I won't. You deserve to fail and it's not my fault. Why am I responsible for you? I was supposed to do your homework for you, help you through, let you cheat off of me because we're best friends. *(Beat.)* Maybe you're not my best friend, though. Maybe a friend wouldn't always ask that kind of thing. It makes me, like, support your problem. So you'll graduate stupid. How does that help? How does that make you my best friend? I know you think I betrayed you, but I can't do this anymore. If that makes you hate me, well, I guess that's just how it will be. *(Beat.)* I'm starting to feel like a sucker for letting you use me for so long. No more. You'll have to find a new nerd to use from now on.

GRASS ROOTS

HUGO

I'd rather not. No. I'm cool. *(Beat.)* No, really, man.

Well, yeah, I am a little scared of getting caught. Plus, I'd like
to keep all my brain cells. *(Beat.)* I don't care if everyone's doing
it. *(Beat.)* Fine, I'm a loser. *(Beat.)* Great. We aren't friends anymore. Whatever. Do you think that hurts me? *(Beat.)* Okay, so
all of you think I'm chicken. Yeah, that clucking is so original.
Only losers do anything they're told to do.

Whatever! Call me all the names you want. I don't need you
guys. *(Beat.)* Maybe I *will* join the chess club. At least they aren't
moronic.

What are you going to do when you get home? Maybe your
parents don't pay any attention to you, but mine do. They will
know what I've been doing. And I'll be screwed for life. I'm too
young to ruin my life. I was planning to at least wait until college for that.

Okay. *(Beat.)* You win. Give it here.

SEATTLE'S WORST

ROCCO

I don't think I can hack it. I heard some guys talking about me today and they were saying that I was hopeless. I can't go back. But, listen, it's okay. I'll just get another job tomorrow. *(Beat.)* I just don't want to be at a place where they talk about you behind your back. *(Beat.)* Yeah, they're evaluating. I know. But it's a lot of pressure.

Try to imagine, just for a moment, what's it's like to have all these orders yelled at you with more and more people coming in, more shouted orders, and here I am, still trying to figure out how the espresso machine works! Customers are getting all pissy then. One lady said to me, "You don't know what you're doing." People brought their orders back because they were wrong. And other people are yelling, "My God, this is taking all day! I have to be at work!" and stuff like that.

I don't want to be a quitter. But sometimes maybe it's better to cut your losses. Admit you're defeated. *(Beat.)* It's just really shitty there and I'm not going back, okay?

THE AUTHOR

Kristen Dabrowski is an actress, writer, acting teacher, singer, and director. Kristen began her career in children's theater and musical theater; since then, her roles have run the gamut from Greek tragedy to contemporary comedies. She received her MFA in Performance from The Oxford School of Drama in Oxford, England. Kristen has performed at several regional, Off-Broadway, and international theaters such as McCarter Theater, Battersea Arts Centre, the John Houseman Theater, and Tricycle Theatre. The actor's life has taken her all over the United States and England. She is a member of the Actors Equity Association. Currently, Kristen teaches acting, voice, and dialect classes in New York City. You can contact the author at monologue madness@yahoo.com.